Other Books by Gladys Conklin

I LIKE CATERPILLARS
Pictures by Barbara Latham

I LIKE BUTTERFLIES
Pictures by Barbara Latham

WE LIKE BUGS
Pictures by Artur Marokvia

IF I WERE A BIRD
Pictures by Artur Marokvia

THE BUG CLUB BOOK
Pictures by Girard Goodenow

I CAUGHT A LIZARD
Pictures by Artur Marokvia

LUCKY LADYBUGS
Pictures by Glen Rounds

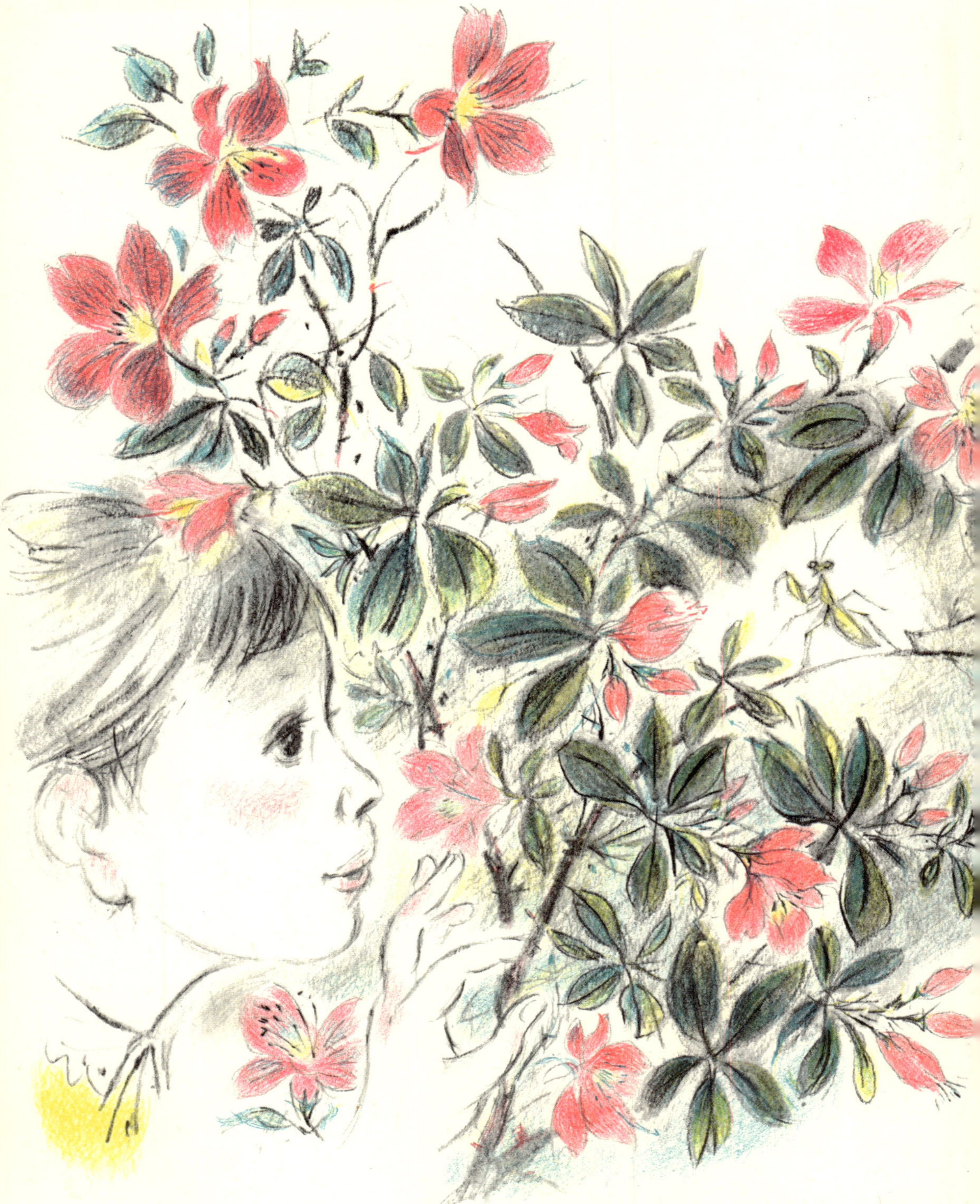

by GLADYS CONKLIN
pictures by ARTUR MAROKVIA

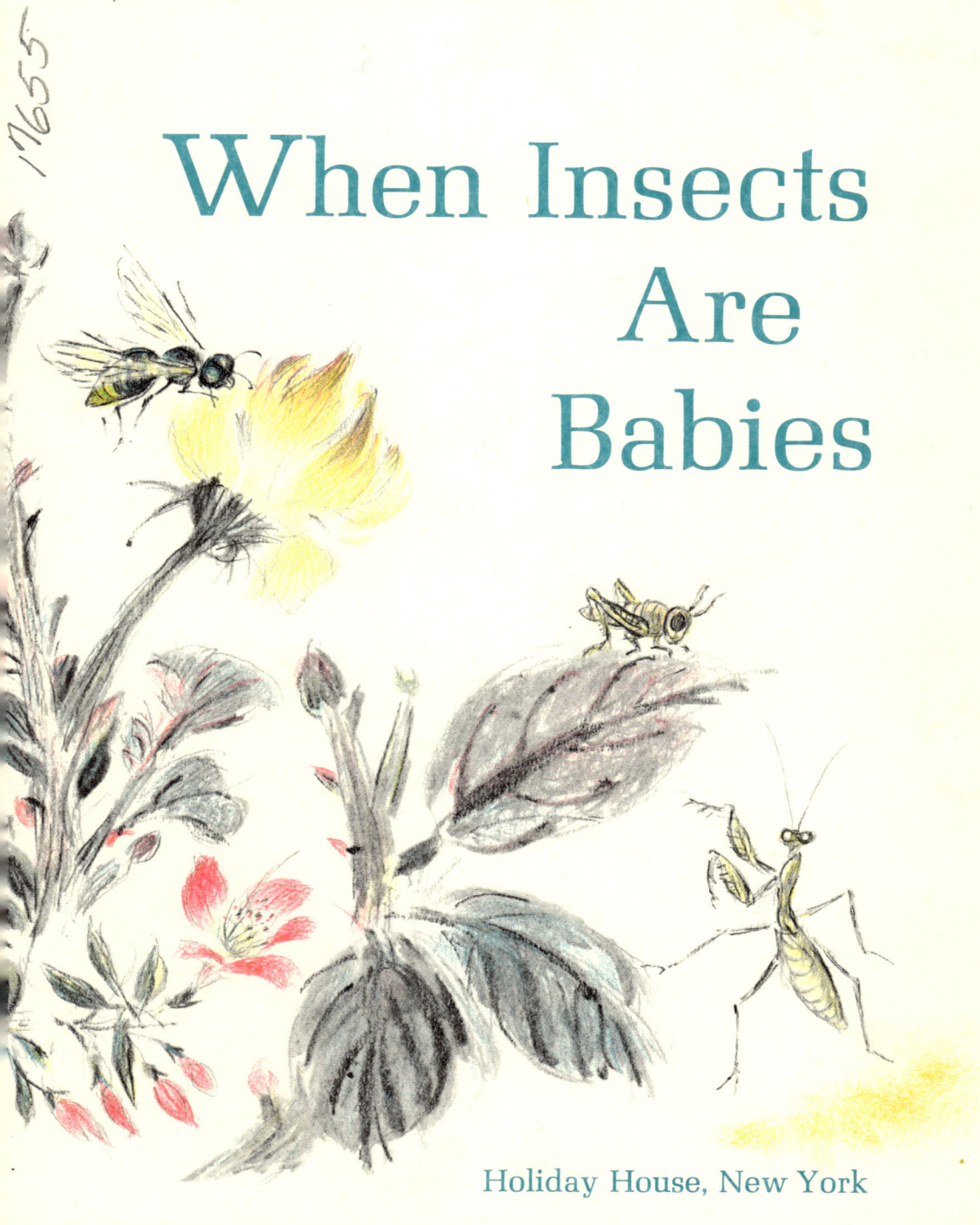

When Insects Are Babies

Holiday House, New York

Text copyright © 1969 by Gladys Conklin
Illustrations copyright © 1969 by Artur Marokvia
All rights reserved
Printed in the United States of America

FOR ED, who didn't have time to write it

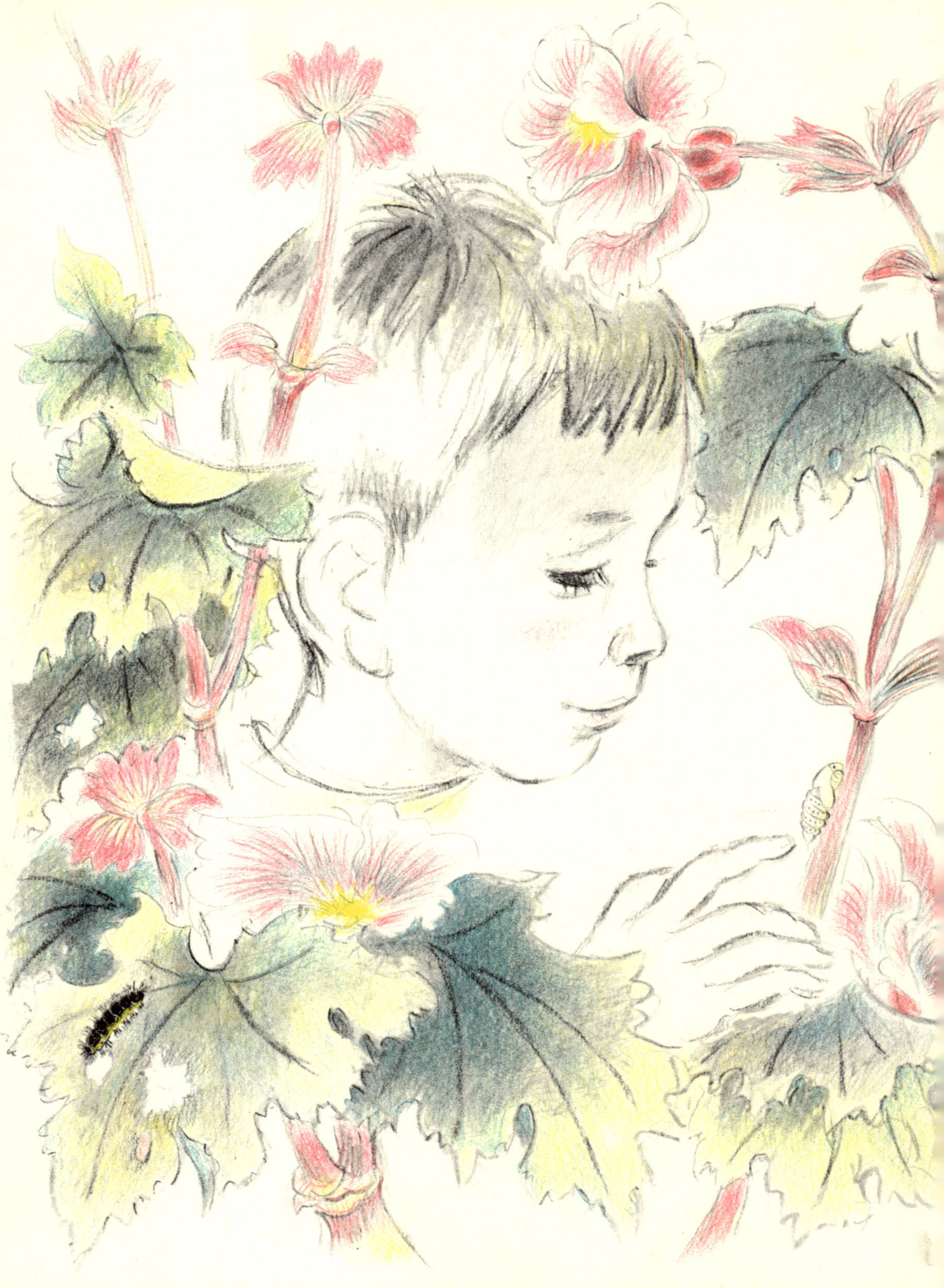

One day I found a funny little bug.
I held it in my hand and looked at it.
It was a new kind to me. I couldn't
guess what it was. But I wanted
to find out.

There are many baby insects that
don't look like their parents.
They're not the same shape.
They don't eat the same kind of food.
Other baby insects do look like their
parents. But they have no wings.

New baby insects are tiny. Many times
I don't see them until I look again.

I found a praying mantis egg case
on a bush. I brought it home
and put it in the garden.
When it hatched, hundreds of little
mantises came tumbling out.

Baby mantises look like their parents, but they have no wings. They eat tiny green bugs called aphids.
As they grow bigger, they eat bigger insects like grasshoppers and katydids. It takes about two months for them to grow up and have wings.

I saw some white bubbles in the grass.
I took a straw and stirred them.
A strange little bug was hiding in there.
When I uncovered him, he made more bubbles to hide in.

A baby spittlebug lives in the
bubbles. His body is soft, and
he stays in the bubbles all the time he's
growing up. All spittlebugs suck
juice from the grass stems. When the
young ones grow up and have wings, they fly
from bush to bush.

Baby beetles are hard to find.
A baby pine sawyer
looks like a soft white caterpillar.

The mother beetle lays her eggs
in the cracks of old or dead trees.
The eggs hatch and the baby pine sawyers
eat their way into the soft wood.
They grow big and fat. Then they
change into beetles with very long feelers.

There's a bright green beetle
out in the field. It runs so fast
I can't catch it. When I get too close,
it spreads its wings and flies.

A baby tiger beetle lives in a hole in the ground. It catches small insects that come near its hole. It lives in the ground all winter. In the spring it comes out as a bright green tiger beetle.

On hot summer days we fill our pockets with empty cicada shells. The tree trunks are covered with them. Hundreds of young cicadas come out of the ground at one time. They climb up the trees and leave their baby clothes sticking to the bark.

The mother cicada lays her eggs on
the twigs of trees. The eggs hatch
and the young cicadas fall to the ground.
They dig down to the roots.
These roots are their food until they
come out of the ground.

There's a big gray paper nest in the woods. It's full of hornets. I like to watch the busy hornets come and go. If I get too close, a hornet will buzz near me. I run away, because hornets sting very hard.

The hornet chews bits of old wood and changes it into soft gray paper. She builds a nursery for her babies. In the center is a nest for her eggs. When the eggs hatch, she feeds the babies small insects and fruit juice.

I saw a black wasp dragging a
caterpillar over the ground.
I stood still and watched.
The wasp came to a small hole
and took the caterpillar inside.
When the wasp came out,
she scratched dirt over the hole.

Inside the hole, the wasp lays one egg on the caterpillar. When the egg hatches, the fresh caterpillar is there for the baby wasp to eat. The baby grows fast and soon turns into a black wasp with wings. It digs out of the hole and flies away.

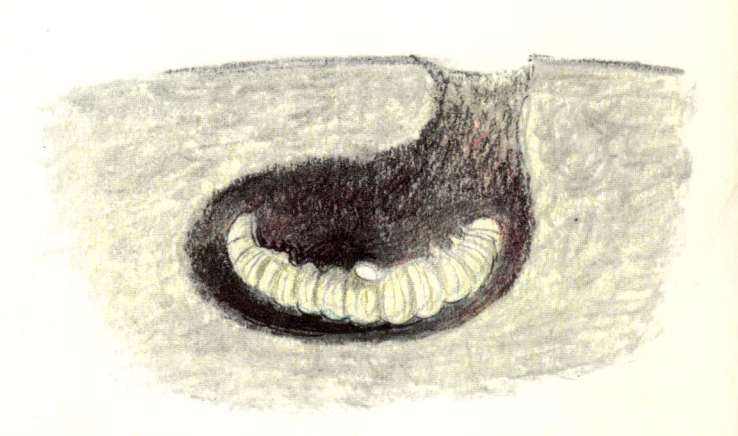

We watch a bumblebee working in the flowers. She has two hairy yellow baskets on her hind legs. If we stand quietly, she won't sting us. We can't find her nest. It may be under a log or in a hole in the ground.

The bumblebee takes care of her eggs and guards them. They hatch into tiny babies. The mother feeds them honey and pollen which she gathers from the flowers. When the young bees grow up, they will help their mother feed many more small babies.

There are many interesting things in the pond. Sometimes I see little tubes moving around in the shallow water. They look like sticks, but there are tiny little legs moving out in front.

The caddis fly lives near ponds and streams. She drops her eggs into the water. When they hatch, each baby builds a tube of sticks or pebbles that protects its soft body. They crawl around eating small water animals and tiny plants. In the spring they come out of the water as grown-up caddis flies.

One day we saw a fat little brownish twig
move along the branch of a tree.
It was moved by six tiny legs.
Some kind of insect was hiding
under the bits of dried leaf.

The bagworm builds a silk case around itself. By the fall it has grown up and lays eggs in the case. As soon as the eggs hatch, the tiny caterpillars crawl out of the case. Each makes its own case of silk and covers it with bits of leaves.
They move around hunting for fresh leaves to eat.

We don't like the earwigs in our garden. They eat the lettuce leaves and the rose petals.
They have pinchers on the back ends of their bodies, but they never pinch us.

The earwig guards her eggs.
She protects her babies until they
are able to take care of themselves.
They hide in the flower blossoms
during the day and come out
at night to eat.

Baby grasshoppers look like their parents, but they can't fly. I caught one and held him in my hand. I let him hop down and watched him wash his funny face. He licked his front feet and rubbed them over his face and big eyes.

A grasshopper lays her eggs in the ground. The young hatch in the spring and dig their way out. They're so small that not many people see them. They climb up the grass stems and start eating. When they get their wings and can fly, they still eat grass.

I saw something move on a blade of grass. It looked like a tiny little lizard. It was eating soft green bugs. I watched it pick up a bug with its sharp jaws and eat it.

One day this little "lizard" spins a tiny silk ball. It curls up inside for a few days. There it changes into a green lacewing. She pushes open a door and comes out. She lays her eggs on a leaf. Each egg is fastened to the end of a thread. The eggs hatch into lacewing babies that look like tiny little lizards.

We watch the dragonflies at the pond.
They zoom and dive like little
jet planes. They are catching mosquitoes.
The mother dragonfly dips down and
drops her eggs into the water.

The eggs hatch into baby dragonflies.
They live in the water for two or
three years. They eat tadpoles and
small fish. One day they stop eating
and crawl up the stem of a water plant.
The skin dries and splits down the back.
Out comes an adult dragonfly with wings.

We like to run outdoors
after dark and catch fireflies.
Five or six in a jar make a
fairy lantern in our room.
Flash! Off! Flash! Off!
goes the wonderful light.

The young fireflies live in the ground. They give a faint glow as they move through the wet earth. They eat earthworms and soft insects. For two years they eat and grow. At last they can fly. They come out of the ground and join the dance of lights
in the meadow.

I found a small furry moth
on a leaf. I picked the leaf and
put it in a jar. The next morning
there were dozens of tiny yellow eggs
laid in straight rows.

The eggs hatched into tiny caterpillars.
They are the babies of the woolly bear moth.
I put three in a jar. They're easy
to feed. They eat weeds and garden
flowers. I watch them weave silk tents
around themselves. They sleep all
winter. In the spring they come out
as small furry moths.

Baby insects are fun to watch.
They are hard to find and often
we don't know what they are.
We want to find out, so we put
one in a jar and raise it.
We give it fresh food every day.
Some baby insects grow up in two months.
Some take six months. One morning we
look and the baby insect is grown up.
Now we know what it is.